To

_____

From

_____

Date

_____

Jesus Listens for Christmas: 25 Prayers and Devotions for Kids

© 2025 Jesus Calling Foundation

Tommy Nelson, PO Box 141000, Nashville, TN 37214

Text adapted from *Jesus Listens: 365 Prayers for Kids* and *Jesus Listens for Advent and Christmas: Prayers for the Season.*

Published in Nashville, Tennessee, by Tommy Nelson. Tommy Nelson is an imprint of Thomas Nelson. Thomas Nelson is a registered trademark of HarperCollins Christian Publishing, Inc.

Tommy Nelson titles may be purchased in bulk for educational, business, fundraising, or sales promotional use. For information, please email SpecialMarkets@ThomasNelson.com.

ISBN 978-1-4002-5344-9 (audiobook)
ISBN 978-1-4002-5351-7 (eBook)
ISBN 978-1-4002-5340-1 (HC)

Library of Congress Control Number: 2025001446

Written by Sarah Young
Adapted by Kris Bearss
Illustrated by Sally Wilson

Printed in India

25 26 27 28 29   NT   10 9 8 7 6 5 4 3 2 1

Mfr: NT / India City: Faridabad, India / August 2025 / PO #12283868

Jesus Listens
for Christmas

25 Prayers
& Devotions for Kids

Sarah Young

illustrated by Sally Wilson

Tommy NELSON®

An Imprint of Thomas Nelson
thomasnelson.com

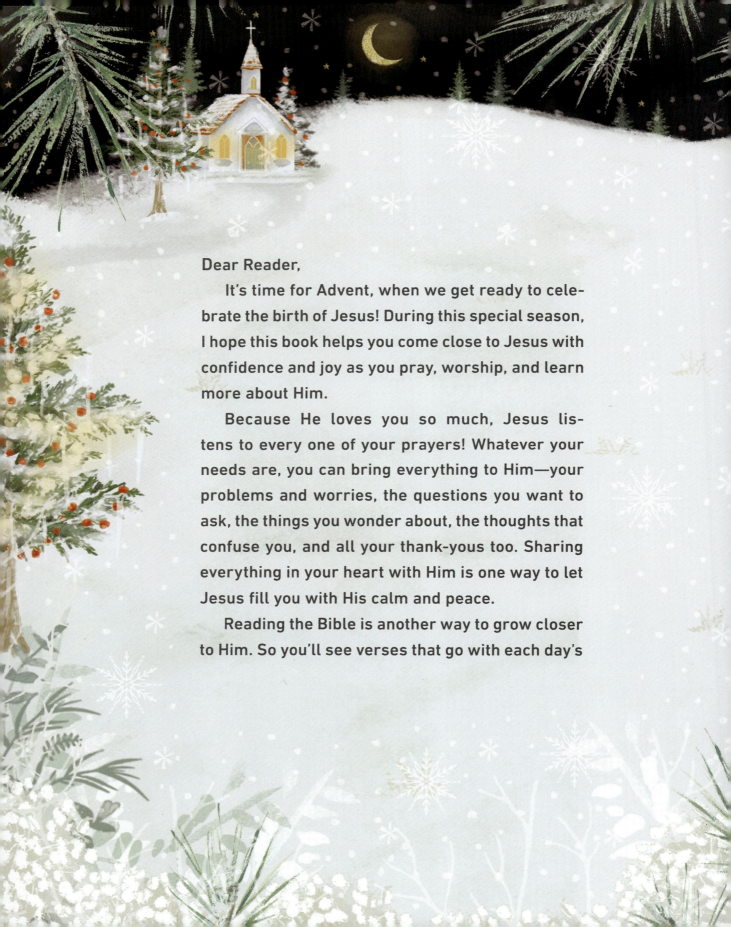

Dear Reader,

It's time for Advent, when we get ready to celebrate the birth of Jesus! During this special season, I hope this book helps you come close to Jesus with confidence and joy as you pray, worship, and learn more about Him.

Because He loves you so much, Jesus listens to every one of your prayers! Whatever your needs are, you can bring everything to Him—your problems and worries, the questions you want to ask, the things you wonder about, the thoughts that confuse you, and all your thank-yous too. Sharing everything in your heart with Him is one way to let Jesus fill you with His calm and peace.

Reading the Bible is another way to grow closer to Him. So you'll see verses that go with each day's

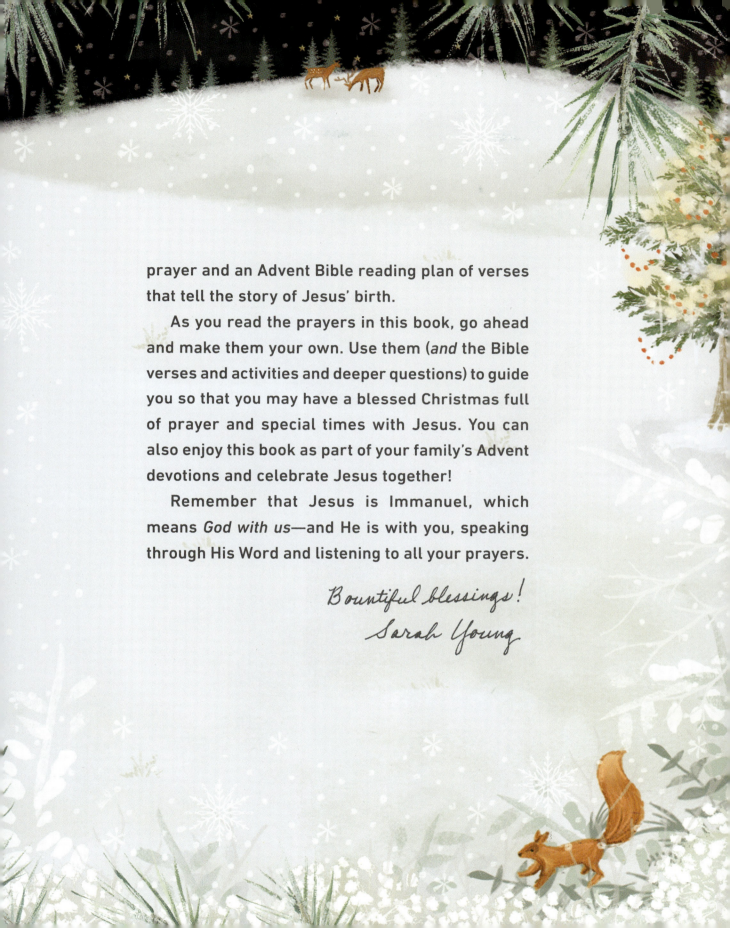

prayer and an Advent Bible reading plan of verses that tell the story of Jesus' birth.

As you read the prayers in this book, go ahead and make them your own. Use them (*and* the Bible verses and activities and deeper questions) to guide you so that you may have a blessed Christmas full of prayer and special times with Jesus. You can also enjoy this book as part of your family's Advent devotions and celebrate Jesus together!

Remember that Jesus is Immanuel, which means *God with us*—and He is with you, speaking through His Word and listening to all your prayers.

Bountiful blessings!

Sarah Young

DAY 1

WHAT THE SHEPHERDS SAW

Suddenly a great army of heaven's angels appeared with the angel, singing praises to God: "Glory to God in the highest heaven, and peace on earth to those with whom he is pleased!"

—Luke 2:13–14 GNT

Dear Jesus,

Christmas is coming! I want to be ready to celebrate the miracles of Your birth and Your life here on Earth. Even though You are God, You *became a human and lived among us*. You left heaven and made Your home on this planet.

I like to imagine what the *shepherds* saw the night You were born. They *were out in the fields* near Bethlehem, *watching over their sheep*. Suddenly, an angel appeared to them! He told them that You had been born. Then many angels came from heaven and lit up the sky with the light of Your glory. All the angels were *singing praises to God*, saying: *"Glory to God in the highest heaven, and peace on earth to those with whom He is pleased!"*

It is good to think about the glory of Your birth, Jesus. The shepherds must have been so surprised and so happy to hear the angel's good news. You are amazing—and I worship You!

In Your marvelous Name, Jesus, *Amen*

John 1:14 NCV; Luke 2:8

Activity

Does your family have a calendar? It probably has lots of events in December! With a colored highlighter, write *Jesus* across the calendar page. Now when anyone checks the schedule, they will remember to celebrate Jesus—the reason for this special season—each and every day.

Advent Bible Reading
John 1:1–4

DAY 2

NEW STRENGTH

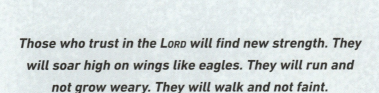

Those who trust in the Lᴏʀᴅ will find new strength. They
will soar high on wings like eagles. They will run and
not grow weary. They will walk and not faint.

—Isaiah 40:31 ɴʟᴛ

Dear Jesus,

My days are so busy! And during the Christmas season, there are even
more things to do than usual: special school and church activities, shopping
for gifts, baking, decorating, traveling to visit family. In this busy, busy time,
please help me make time for You and remember that Christmas is really
all about *You*, Jesus. I love spending time with You!

It's easy to get worn out with all the excitement of the holidays. So
please remind me to *come to You when I'm tired*. I can rest in Your Presence
and tell You all my troubles. I love hearing You whisper, "I am with you"
during our quiet times together. And I praise You for the way You give me
new strength whenever I spend time with You. Thank You, Lord!

In Your strong Name, Jesus, *Amen*

Matthew 11:28; Psalm 105:4 ɴʟᴛ

Talk to God about how He gives you His strength as you create an eagle
mask. Cut eye holes in a paper plate, and cover the plate with bits of
colored paper. Glue on a triangle for the beak.

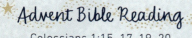

Colossians 1:15–17, 19–20

DAY 3

A FOREVER KIND OF JOY

God has said, "I will never leave you; I will never abandon you."

—Hebrews 13:5

Dear Jesus,

Sometimes I try to find my happiness in things and events. That's silly, I know—because none of that stuff lasts. Even the very best Christmas gift gets old, and the very best Christmas vacation ends.

Sometimes I wish I could just "stop the clock" and keep things as they are, but I can't. Your Presence, though, is a blessing that will go on and on, giving me joy forever. I'm so happy You've promised that *You will never leave me*.

Your best blessings are the kind that never end. I know that You also give me gifts for right now—like my friends and clothes and toys. But they're not the gifts I need most. If I want the kind of joy that never goes away, I need to stay close to You, Jesus. Because it's *being with You that fills me with Your forever kind of joy*.

In Your joy-filled Name, Jesus, *Amen*

Psalm 16:11; Deuteronomy 30:20

Activity

Being with Jesus is the gift that never ends. When you wake up this Saturday, set a timer to sound every hour until you go to bed. When the timer goes off, stop what you're doing and thank Jesus out loud for one of His forever gifts.

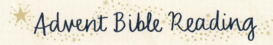

Advent Bible Reading

Jeremiah 33:14–16; Micah 5:2, 4

DAY 4

ONE HUNDRED PERCENT GOOD

Jesus answered, "I tell you the truth. Before Abraham was born, I am!"

—John 8:58

Dear Jesus,

At this time of year when many people are focused on gifts, I want to take time to think about all the different blessings You give me. So I'm stopping right now to say: "*Thank You, Lord, because You are good. Your Love continues forever.*" Thank You for the gift of life—every breath I breathe is a blessing from You. I'm also thankful for Your everyday blessings, like food and water, a home, clothes, and people who love me.

But the greatest gift of all is the one You give me because I trust You as my Savior. That gift is forgiveness of *all* my sins. You have washed away the dirt of every lie I've told, every mean word I've said, every unkind thought I've had, and every wrong thing I've done. And one day, I look forward to Life forever with You in heaven!

As I think about how much You do for me, I find joy in knowing who You are—the great *I Am*! You are one hundred percent good. There isn't even a tiny speck of bad in You. You give Your goodness to *the world* in Your Love that goes on and on forever!

Thank You for always being with me and for *Your Love that never fails me.*

In Your blessed Name, Jesus, *Amen*

Psalm 107:1; Psalm 106:1 CEV

Instead of a Christmas *wish* list, create a *gift* list. Make a list of the gifts Jesus has given you. Write little things, like a joke; big gifts, like your favorite Bible verse; and ways Jesus has taken care of you.

Advent Bible Reading

Isaiah 11:1–5, 10

YOU ARE ENOUGH

"She will give birth to a son, and they will call him Immanuel, which means 'God is with us.'"

—Matthew 1:23 NLT

Dear Jesus,

You are *Immanuel. This name means "God is with us."* And this name of Yours tells me that You *are* enough—You're all I need!

That's pretty easy to believe when things in my life are going just the way I want. But when I run into tough times—especially when problems show up one right after the other—I sometimes start to wonder if You really *are* taking care of me. Before I know it, my mind is spinning, spinning, spinning while I try to figure out how *I* can make things better.

Instead of thinking about my problems so much, I need to remember that *You are always with me.* I'm so thankful that You're ready to help me through even my biggest problems. No matter what's happening, You will see me through my troubles as long as I keep turning to You for help. I choose to *be joyful and glad, because You are my Savior*—You are the God who saves me.

In Your saving Name, Jesus, *Amen*

Matthew 28:20; Habakkuk 3:17–18 GNT

Reflection

Problems don't go away just because it's Christmas, do they? When you feel worried or upset, remind yourself: *Jesus is with me.* You can ask Him for help with *anything.* He is all you need.

Advent Bible Reading

John 3:16–17

Activity

Go get your sunglasses. Now put them on while standing in front of a
lit Christmas tree. Even the darkest sunglasses cannot overpower the
lights on the tree, can they? Imagine how much brighter Jesus shines
as the Light of the World!

DAY 6

YOU SHINE THROUGH THE DARKNESS

Before the world was made, God decided to make
us his own children through Jesus Christ.

—Ephesians 1:5

Dear Jesus,

The Bible says that *You are the Light of the World*. Like a light, You help me see the truth of Your Word. At Christmastime, we worship You for coming into this world as a baby to help us clearly see the darkness of sin and the brightness of life with You.

One way I like to celebrate Your birth is by looking at the lights on a Christmas tree. Those lights remind me to think about why You came to Earth, Jesus. You are the Light that shines forever. You break through the darkness of evil, showing the way to heaven for everyone who is sorry for their sins and trusts in You.

The Bible says that *Your Light shines in the darkness. And the darkness has not overpowered the Light*—Your Light is *so* much more powerful than sin's darkness! That's why I need to *keep my eyes on You*, Jesus. You give me the help and hope I need to stay in Your Light. You comfort me with this wonderful promise: *"The person who follows Me will have the Light that gives Life."*

Thank You, Lord, that nothing can change Your plan to save Your people. You promise that everyone who trusts You to be their Savior will live with You forever!

In Your shining Name, Jesus, *Amen*

John 8:12; John 1:5; Hebrews 12:2 NLT

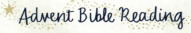
Advent Bible Reading
Isaiah 61:1–3

DAY 7

SO MANY BLESSINGS

God, your love is so precious!

—Psalm 36:7

Dear Jesus,

You are the God who created all the little things, like the design of each snowflake and butterfly wing. You are the God who made a universe so huge we can't count all its stars. *And* You are the God who cares so much about every detail of my life that You answer my prayers very carefully! You even care if I stub my toe or if my hands are cold.

The Bible tells me to *never stop praying*. I'm happy that You listen to all my prayers. I'm learning that the more I pray, the more I see Your answers. This helps me trust You more.

I praise You for Your unlimited Love. I don't ever have to worry about You running out of anything. I can ask You for whatever I need and then wait joyfully for You to help me. And You often give me even more than I ask for!

Like receiving gifts on Christmas morning, I am ready for all the good things You have to give me. But most of all, I open up my heart and my hands to *You*. Thank You, Lord!

In Your great Name, Jesus, *Amen*

1 Thessalonians 5:17; Psalm 36:5–6

Activity

To make a snowflake decoration, fold a piece of white paper in half. Fold the paper in half again, and cut off one side to make a square. Cut small and big triangles into each side of the square. Open the paper to see your one-of-a-kind snowflake!

Advent Bible Reading

John 1:9–12

TEACH ME TO WAIT

Show me how to live. Guide me in your truth.
Teach me, my God, my Savior.

—Psalm 25:4–5

Dear Jesus,

Advent is a season of waiting. A season of waiting in hope to celebrate Your birth in Bethlehem!

Lord, You know I'm not so good at waiting. I like to make plans and make things happen. But You've been teaching me that You are God, and You have wisely decided that there's a time to do those things—and there is also a time to wait. A time to sit and talk to You and read Your Word and trust Your plans.

As hard as waiting is for me, spending time with You makes me feel better. You give me many blessings through our time together. Many of the good things You've promised are in the future—just like God's promise of Your birth to His people long ago. While I'm resting in Your Presence, You're preparing me for my future blessings. I can't see them clearly yet, but I'm trusting that they are there.

When I'm struggling to wait patiently—wondering why I have to wait so long for good news—remind me to put my *trust in You*. You will *show me how to live* and *guide me in Your truth*.

In Your hope-filled Name, Jesus, *Amen*

Psalm 40:1; Psalm 143:8

Make a birthday gift for Jesus. Draw a picture, practice a song, or prepare to act out a Bible story. Then, when it's time to open gifts light a birthday candle, sing "Happy Birthday," and show your family your gift for Jesus. He will love it!

Advent Bible Reading

John 1:14, 16–18

DAY 9

LORD, YOU'RE WAITING TOO

The Lord wants to show his mercy to you. He
wants to rise and comfort you.

—Isaiah 30:18

Dear Jesus,

I'm grateful that *Your mercies never stop. They are new every morning.* I can begin each day with confidence because I know that Your endless supply of blessings is waiting for me—even if I messed up yesterday or things didn't go how I planned.

I know that You hear all my prayers. Not a single one slips by You. This helps me wait for Your answers and not give up.

Even though You haven't answered some of my prayers yet, I trust that You know what You're doing. You keep all Your promises in Your own perfect way and Your own perfect timing. Thank You, Jesus, for coming into the world that first Christmas Day to give me Your Peace. If I get tired of waiting, please remind me that *You* are waiting too—waiting to *show me Your mercy and comfort.* You wait for just the right time to bless me with all the things You've lovingly prepared for me.

In Your faithful Name, Jesus, *Amen*

Lamentations 3:22–23; John 14:27

Reflection

Jesus hears all your prayers. Sometimes He says yes right away. Sometimes He says no so that He can give you something even better. Sometimes He tells you to wait. Whether He says *yes*, *no*, or *wait*, you can be sure that He is looking out for you.

Advent Bible Reading
Isaiah 9:6–7

DAY 10
YOU ARE THE LORD OF PEACE

We pray that the Lord of peace will give you peace at all times and in every way. May the Lord be with all of you.

—2 Thessalonians 3:16

Dear Jesus,

Sometimes I wish I could understand everything. But You teach me that even if I could read all the books in the world, I'd still never find peace. The only way to have peace is *to trust You with all my heart instead of depending on my own understanding.*

I have to admit, that's not so easy for me to do! I love figuring things out. The trouble is, this world keeps throwing problems at me like they are snowballs. As soon as I figure out one problem, another one comes flying at me. Soon my mind is racing, trying to figure out the answer to this new problem. But what I really need to be doing is looking for *You,* the One who understands everything and is always in control.

Thank You that Your Peace is really *not* hard to find. And neither are You! Because I belong to You, You wrap me up in the blanket of peace that comes from living close to You. I'm so thankful that I always have You with me, Jesus. The more I trust You, the more of Your precious Peace You give me!

In Your perfect Name, Jesus, *Amen*

Proverbs 3:5; Romans 5:1

Activity

Wrap your favorite blanket around your shoulders. Notice the warmth and softness as you imagine Jesus wrapping His Peace around you. Talk with Him about your troubles. Then listen. Is His Spirit comforting you with a Bible verse or the words of a song about Him?

Advent Bible Reading
Luke 1:5–14, 17

DAY 11

EVERYTHING IS POSSIBLE

Jesus looked straight at them and said, "For people this is impossible. But for God all things are possible."

—Mark 10:27

Dear Jesus,

With decorations, music, and yummy smells all around at Christmastime, I'm thankful I can experience so many wonderful things with my senses. But You are teaching me to search deeper and higher. You want me to *live by what I believe about You and Your power, not just by what I can see,* hear, smell, or touch.

One of your powerful promises is that *all things are possible with You!* When it looks like the bad guys are winning or a problem is too big to be fixed, it's easy for me to get caught up in the details and forget about You. I'm sorry, Lord. Help me focus on You and all that You can do.

When You lived on Earth as a man, *Your miracles showed that You are Christ,* the Son of God. Even the miracle of Your birth proved it! I'm thankful that You're still doing miracles today. All things are possible with You!

In Your powerful Name, Jesus, *Amen*

2 Corinthians 5:7; John 10:24–25

Reflection

Which miracles from the Bible can you remember? When did you pray for Jesus to help you and He did? Worship and praise Him as these memories come to mind.

Advent Bible Reading

Luke 1:18–25

EVEN IN THE NOISIEST PLACES

*"You will call my name. You will come to me and
pray to me. And I will listen to you."*

—Jeremiah 29:12

Dear Jesus,

I love to hear You whisper this promise again and again: *"I am with you.
I am with you. I am with you."* It's sad that some people never hear Your
whispers. That's because they hardly ever *search for You with their whole
heart*—not even at Christmastime, when songs and stories of You are every-
where. But I know that You are always near, constantly watching over me.

Anytime I want to be with You, I just need to find a quiet place where I
won't be pulled away by other things that distract me. There, I can open up
the pages of my Bible or sing songs about You. Someday, with lots of practice
and with Your help, I'll know how to carry that quiet place in my heart. Then
I can take Your words with me wherever I go, even into the noisiest places.

I'm still new at listening to You, but even now, I can sometimes hear You
whisper Your promise as I go through my noisy day: "I am with you. I am
with you. I am with you."

Jesus, I rejoice in You!

In Your wonderful Name, Jesus, *Amen*

Isaiah 41:10; Jeremiah 29:13

Reflection

Where is a quiet place you can go to spend time with Jesus? Go there
now to read your Bible, sing to Him, pray, and thank Him that He is
always with you.

Advent Bible Reading
Matthew 1:23, Luke 1:26–38

DAY 13

LITTLE TASTES OF HEAVEN

[Christ] gave up his place with God and made himself nothing.
He was born as a man and became like a servant.

—Philippians 2:7

Dear Jesus,

When I sit in Your Presence, *You shine Your Light into my heart, letting me know a little of Your Glory.* I can't imagine how much You gave up when You left heaven and came to Earth as a helpless baby. No other king would ever give up his castle! But You gave up Your home in heaven so You could understand what it's like to be human—what it's like to be *me*.

And if that wasn't enough, You chose to be born in a stable with a feeding trough for Your crib, even though You are God. There was nothing glorious or beautiful about that! Still, the angels lit up the skies as they announced "Glory!" to the amazed shepherds who were out in the fields.

Jesus, You left heaven to come to Earth, just as God Your Father planned. And when I sit with You, I get to experience just a tiny bit of heaven. The closer I get to You, the more You bless me with little tastes of how wonderful heaven will be! Lord, I praise Your holy Name!

In Your holy Name, Jesus, *Amen*

2 Corinthians 4:6; Luke 2:13–14

Draw or paint a picture of heaven. Use bright colors and other materials such as glitter, stickers, and confetti to make it sparkle. Be sure to include Jesus, because His Presence lights up the whole place!

Luke 1:39–42, 44–55

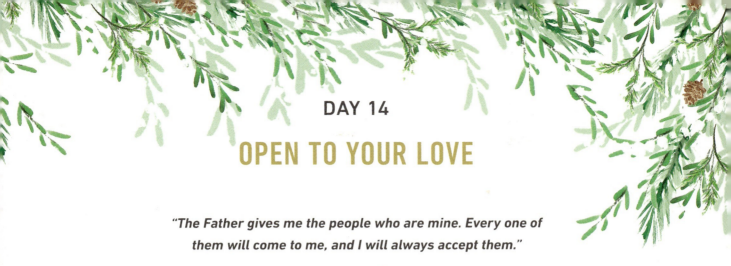

DAY 14

OPEN TO YOUR LOVE

"The Father gives me the people who are mine. Every one of them will come to me, and I will always accept them."

—John 6:37

Dear Jesus,

As I read my Bible this December day, I can hear You calling me to come closer. When my mind and heart are quiet, it's like I'm hearing a holy whisper: *"Come to Me. Come to Me. Come to Me."*

I open my heart to You and let go of my fears and worries. I let them melt away like snowflakes. As my worries disappear, I feel Your Love pulling me close to You, Lord.

Please help me, through *Your Holy Spirit,* to really open my heart to Your Love and Presence. I want to *be filled with more and more of You* so that I can give more and more of You to others. Although Your Love is too huge to be measured or explained, I can know what it's like to have perfect love in my life—because that's how You love me!

In Your amazing Name, Jesus, *Amen*

Matthew 11:28; James 4:8 NLT; Ephesians 3:16–17, 19

Reflection

Reading the Bible is one way you can open your heart to Jesus and be filled with more of Him. What else can you do today to show Jesus that you love Him and want to be close to Him?

Advent Bible Reading

Luke 1:57–65

DAY 15

REASONS TO BE GLAD

Thank the Lord because he is good. His love continues forever.

—Psalm 118:1

Dear Jesus,

This is the day that You have made! That's all the reason I need to *rejoice and be glad*. But You don't stop there! You fill my day with blessings and with so many chances to grow closer to You.

I want to go through this whole day with You as if Christmas was here already—opening up all the smiles and surprises You've planned for me. And I want to thank You for every single one! Every day, I can *thank You because You are good, and Your Love continues forever.*

When I'm thankful, I can walk through the hardest, darkest day with joy in my heart. That's because I know that *the Light of Your Presence* is still shining on me, like the star that led the wise men as they traveled to see You. I'm so grateful for You, Jesus, the Friend who is always by my side.

In Your bright and beautiful Name, Jesus, *Amen*

Psalm 118:24; Psalm 89:15–16

A candy cane can remind us of Jesus. The red stripes stand for Jesus' blood, which He shed on the cross to take away our sins. And the white stripes remind us of how pure and perfect He is.

Draw and color a candy cane. Roll up the paper like a scroll, and tie a real candy cane to it with a ribbon. Then put it in a family member's Christmas stocking.

Luke 1:67–80; John 1:7–8

NOTHING BETTER

Let everything that breathes praise the Lord. Praise the Lord!

—Psalm 150:6

Dear Jesus,

I praise You because Your Love is better than anything—even better than life! There's no limit to Your Love either. That makes me so happy! Your Love is greater than anyone else's love. There's always more of it than I can ever dream of. And it never ends.

Your precious Love makes my life so much better in so many ways. No matter what else happens, I can count on You because You love me perfectly. Knowing that You love me like this helps me love others more. And it helps me grow into the person You created me to be.

As I think about *how wide and how long and how high and how deep Your Love is*, I just have to stop and worship You. The psalm says, *Let everything that breathes praise You, Lord*. And as Christmas Day approaches, that's what I say too!

In Your loving Name, Jesus, *Amen*

Psalm 63:3; Ephesians 3:18

This Advent season, love others with the same love Jesus gives you. Look for ways to help, comfort, and be kind. If anyone asks, "Why are you being so nice?" tell them: "Because Jesus loves you, just like He loves me."

Matthew 1:18–25

DAY 17

THE INVITATION

The Lord . . . said, "I love you people with a love that will last forever. I became your friend because of my love and kindness."

—Jeremiah 31:3

Dear Jesus,

You are always inviting me closer to You. You came to Earth as a baby so that I could be friends with You. I love to hear You whispering in my heart, "*Come to Me*, dear child. *I love you forever.*"

Jesus, I like to say yes to Your invitation by *thinking about You*. One of my favorite things to think about is the wonderful truth that *You are always with me*. It's one of my favorites because this world is changing all the time. My friends change, my teams change, my schools change—even *I'm* changing as I learn and grow up and get bigger. But *You* never change. I can count on You to be *the same* loving, wise, and ready-to-help Lord that You have always been.

I'm learning that the closer to You I live, the happier I am. You bless me with Your Joy and help me bring joy to others.

In Your blessed Name, Jesus, *Amen*

Hebrews 3:1; Psalm 73:23

Make an ornament to remind you that Jesus is always with you. Draw a big star and a little star on a piece of cardboard. Cut out the stars and color them. Then paste the small star on top of the large star. Hang the ornament with a string.

Luke 2:1–7

DAY 18

THE MOST WONDERFUL TREASURE!

God . . . made the world through the Son.

—Hebrews 1:2

Dear Jesus,

As I celebrate Your birth this Christmas, help me remember that You are God.

The Bible says *You are the Word that became a man and lived with us.* You are also the Savior, who is God Almighty! If You were only a man, Your life and death would not have been enough to save me from my sins. But because You are also God, You have the power to save me. What a great truth to celebrate! It's so amazing that You—the One who was born into the world as a tiny, helpless baby—are the very same God who created this whole world!

Even though You were rich in heaven, You became poor on Earth to help me. You became poor so that I could become rich in Your blessings. No Christmas present in the whole world could ever be as awesome as the treasure I have in You, Jesus. Because of You, my sins can be *taken away as far as the east is from the west.* Thank You, Lord, for this awesome gift!

In Your amazing Name, Jesus, *Amen*

John 1:1, 14; 2 Corinthians 8:9 NLT; Psalm 103:12

Jesus came to Earth to forgive you. What sin do you need His forgiveness for? Draw or write it with a pencil on paper or a marker on a dry-erase board. Then erase it as you say, "I'm sorry, Jesus. Thank You for making this sin disappear as if it never even happened. I love You!"

Luke 2:8–20

DAY 19

HOLDING ON TO HOPE

"Don't be frightened, Mary," the angel told her, "for God has decided to wonderfully bless you! Very soon now, you will become pregnant and have a baby boy, and you are to name him 'Jesus.'"

—Luke 1:30–31 TLB

Dear Jesus,

One of the best parts of the Christmas story is how Mary trusted that You would be born, just because God promised it. Help me trust You like that. *You are faithful—You will do what You promise.*

Some days, I forget to trust You and I worry—especially when lots of things are going wrong. On those days, all I can do is hold on to You by remembering Your promises to always be with me and to answer my prayers. When I don't know what to do, what I really need is to *come and talk with You* and tell You that *You are my hope.* That means trusting You and believing that You're the answer to everything.

I can be full of hope because I know You keep Your promises. Saying words like "I trust You, Jesus. You are my hope" helps me keep holding on to You. Help me, Lord, to never let go of You!

In Your hope-filled Name, Jesus, *Amen*

Hebrews 10:23 NIRV; Psalm 27:8 NLT; Psalm 39:7

Trace your hand and an adult's hand on paper. Cut out the hands and paste them onto a whole sheet of paper. Write prayers and questions for Jesus on the hands. Remember, Jesus is always with you, listening to your prayers.

Advent Bible Reading

Luke 2:22, 25–33, 36–40

DAY 20

LEAD ME TO YOUR PEACE

A child will be born to us. God will give a son to us. He will be responsible for leading the people. His name will be . . . Prince of Peace.

—Isaiah 9:6

Dear Jesus,

At Christmastime we're supposed to be full of happiness, but sometimes I get into confusing situations, and I feel like I'm in the dark.

I know I'm not the only one though. Many of the adults in the Bible were confused or afraid when they heard how God was preparing for Your birth. And just like them, I need Your Peace.

Anytime things just don't make sense, please help me look to You, Jesus, so that I may see more clearly. As soon as I remember that You're with me, I can find hope and rest, just like Joseph and Mary did when the angel spoke to them.

The Bible teaches me to *be still and know that You are God*. And that's something I need to do every day, whether life is calm or confusing. Each day, I need to stop for a moment and remember that You are *the Prince of Peace*. Every time I do, I find that, after a while, I'm ready *to tell You all my problems*.

Lord, I trust You to show me the way I should go. Please lead me to Your Peace.

In Your worthy Name, Jesus, *Amen*

Psalm 46:10; Psalm 62:8

Activity

Plan a puppet show or simple play to tell the story of Jesus' birth. Invite your friends over for snacks and Christmas games, and finish the party with your performance. Be sure to include the good news that Jesus came to save us from our sins and live with us forever.

Advent Bible Reading

Matthew 2:2–6

DAY 21

YOUR LIGHT IN ME

You are all children of the light and of the day;
we don't belong to darkness and night.

—1 Thessalonians 5:5 NLT

Dear Jesus,

You didn't just *bring* Light into the world. *You came as Light into the world so that whoever believes in You would not stay in darkness*. Nothing can put out Your Light because You are all-powerful!

When I believe in You, Jesus, I become a *child of Light*. Your bright Truth soaks deep down inside me. Your Light helps me see things the way You see them—things in the world *and* things in my heart. Every time Your Spirit shines a light on what's inside of me, He finds the truth. He shows me what pleases You and what doesn't please You. Help me get rid of the things You don't like, Lord. I really want to do the things that make You smile instead.

I'm thankful for Your Light that fills me with joy and helps me see everything more clearly. Because I belong to You, I have Your Light shining in me!

In Your bright Name, Jesus, *Amen*

John 12:46 NCV; John 1:5

Turn off the lights and turn on a flashlight. Shine the flashlight into each corner of the room. What can you see in the light that is hidden in the darkness? Now shine the light at your heart. Say a prayer thanking Jesus for being *your* Light and helping you see truth whenever life gets dark and difficult.

⭐ Advent Bible Reading
Matthew 2:7–12

DAY 22

LOOKING FOR YOU

"My sheep listen to my voice. I know them, and they follow me."

—John 10:27

Dear Jesus,

Being with You fills me with joy! That means I can have joy no matter what's happening around me. As I walk through this day, with Christmas just around the corner, I'm going to be looking for signs of Your Presence. Even though I can't see Your Face the way I can see a friend's face, I *know* You're here with me. The more I look for You, the more I find You. So please help me keep my eyes wide open in the big and little things that happen today. I don't want to miss a single hint of You.

Most of all, I want to fill my mind and heart with Your words in the Bible. That's where You speak to me most clearly. As Your promises soak into my thoughts, You bring me even closer to You. I love to hear You telling me through Your Word: *"Listen to My voice. I know you. Follow Me."*

In Your all-powerful Name, Jesus, *Amen*

Psalm 16:11; Jeremiah 29:13

Reflection

The Bible is one of God's greatest gifts. It is God's message to us. In it, you can read about Jesus' words and actions and the powerful works of God.

When was the last time the Bible reminded you of the Holy Spirit's presence? He is your Helper. Thank Him for always being with you—and then watch for Him today!

Advent Bible Reading

Isaiah 40:9–11

DAY 23

YOU ARE MY JOY

Be full of joy in the Lord always. I will say again, be full of joy.

—Philippians 4:4

Dear Jesus,

You are my Joy! Every time I think, whisper, or say these four words out loud, Your Light shines into my life. Because You're always with me, I can have *the joy of Your Presence* at any time. Even if I've messed up or I'm feeling worried about something, I can open my heart to You by saying, "I love You, Jesus!" I like to think about all the ways You love me and all that You've done for me. Those thoughts fill me with *joy in You*, my Savior.

Not only did You come to Earth to rescue me from my sins, but You died on the cross and rose again. And You promised that *You will come back* to this Earth again one day too. *Then You will take me to be with You so that I can be where You are*—in heaven forever!

In this moment, as I relax with You, I can almost hear You whispering, "Dear child, I am your Joy."

In Your beautiful Name, Jesus, *Amen*

Psalm 21:6 NIV; John 14:3

Choose a favorite Christmas song that reminds you of Jesus, and make up a dance—just for Him—to show how you feel about Him.

Isaiah 52:7; 12:5–6

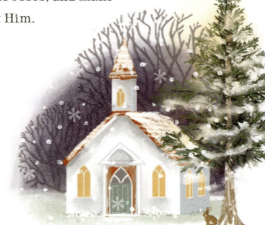

DAY 24

THE ANGEL'S MESSAGE

The angel said to them, "Do not be afraid. I am bringing you
good news that will be a great joy to all the people."

—Luke 2:10 NCV

Dear Jesus,

When an angel appeared to the *shepherds who were in the fields* near Bethlehem, he told them about Your birth. He said, *"Do not be afraid. I am bringing you good news that will be a great joy to all the people."*

The Bible says "Don't be afraid!" over and over again. Thank You, Jesus, for this comforting command. You know I still get scared. *A lot.* But You don't judge me or punish me for being afraid. Instead, You offer me the joy of Your Presence.

The angel's announcement to the shepherds was one of *great* joy: *"Today your Savior was born in the town of David. He is Christ, the Lord"*! I happily *praise You* for the gift of Your Presence—the gift of *Yourself.* Help me to never forget how amazing the good news of the Christmas story is.

In Your wonderful Name, Jesus, *Amen*

Luke 2:8–11 NCV; Psalm 89:15

Use the cardboard from inside a roll of paper towels as a megaphone. Grab an instrument if you have one—a maraca, tambourine, or drum— and march through your home as you announce the happy news of Baby Jesus' birth: "The Savior is born. He is Christ the Lord!"

1 Peter 2:6, 9–10

LIKE THE WISE MEN

When the wise men saw the star, they were filled with joy. They went to the house where the child was and saw him with his mother, Mary. They bowed down and worshiped the child.

—Matthew 2:10–11

Dear Jesus,

You are *the King of all kings and the Lord of all lords*. I worship You for how great and glorious You are! And I come close to You, finding rest in Your loving Presence.

You are both God and Man—the only person who ever lived in this world without sinning. I really need You, Jesus! Only You can save me from my sins *and guide me to the path of peace*. When You were born on that first, long-ago Christmas, You came to give Your life for me.

Today, most of all, I want to *bow down and worship You* like the wise men did. I want to celebrate the amazing miracle of Your birth!

You are my Savior, my Lord, and my King. You gave *everything* to take care of me. I praise You for all that You are—and all You have done!

In Your great and majestic Name, Jesus, *Amen*

1 Timothy 6:15–16; Luke 1:78–79 NLT

Reflection

Jesus is the most wonderful, incredible, fantastic Gift ever! Make time to worship Him today—no matter how busy you are—with presents, yummy food, and seeing family and friends.

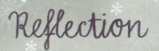

Advent Bible Reading

2 Corinthians 8:9; Philippians 2:5–11

Advent Bible Reading

Anticipation

Day 1: John 1:1–4

Day 2: Colossians 1:15–17, 19–20

Day 3: Jeremiah 33:14–16; Micah 5:2, 4

Day 4: Isaiah 11:1–5, 10

Day 5: John 3:16–17

Day 6: Isaiah 61:1–3

Day 7: John 1:9–12

Day 8: John 1:14, 16–18

Day 9: Isaiah 9:6–7

Revelation

Day 10: Luke 1:5–14, 17

Day 11: Luke 1:18–25

Day 12: Matthew 1:23; Luke 1:26–38

Day 13: Luke 1:39–42, 44–55

Day 14: Luke 1:57–65

Day 15: Luke 1:67–80; John 1:7–8

Day 16: Matthew 1:18–25

Day 17: Luke 2:1–7

Annunciation

Day 18: Luke 2:8–20
Day 19: Luke 2:22, 25–33, 36–40
Day 20: Matthew 2:2–6
Day 21: Matthew 2:7–12

Celebration

Day 22: Isaiah 40:9–11
Day 23: Isaiah 52:7; 12:5–6
Day 24: 1 Peter 2:6, 9–10
Day 25: 2 Corinthians 8:9; Philippians 2:5–11

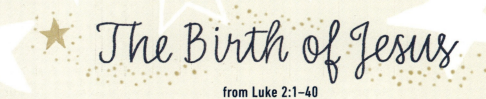

The Birth of Jesus

from Luke 2:1–40

At that time, Augustus Caesar sent an order to all people in the countries that were under Roman rule. The order said that they must list their names in a register. This was the first registration taken while Quirinius was governor of Syria. And everyone went to their own towns to be registered.

So Joseph left Nazareth, a town in Galilee. He went to the town of Bethlehem in Judea. This town was known as the town of David. Joseph went there because he was from the family of David. Joseph registered with Mary because she was engaged to marry him. (Mary was now pregnant.) While Joseph and Mary were in Bethlehem, the time came for her to have the baby. She gave birth to her first son. There were no rooms left in the inn. So she wrapped the baby with cloths and laid him in a box where animals are fed.

SOME SHEPHERDS HEAR ABOUT JESUS

That night, some shepherds were in the fields nearby watching their sheep. An angel of the Lord stood before them. The glory of the Lord was shining around them, and suddenly they became very frightened. The angel said to them, "Don't be afraid, because I am bringing you some good news. It will be a joy to all the people. Today your Savior was born in David's town. He is Christ, the Lord. This is how you will know him: You will find a baby wrapped in cloths and lying in a feeding box."

Then a very large group of angels from heaven joined the first angel. All the angels were praising God, saying:

"Give glory to God in heaven,
and on earth let there be peace to the people who please God."

Then the angels left the shepherds and went back to heaven. The shepherds said to each other, "Let us go to Bethlehem and see this thing that has happened. We will see this thing the Lord told us about."

So the shepherds went quickly and found Mary and Joseph. And the shepherds saw the baby lying in a feeding box. Then they told what the angels had said about this child. Everyone was amazed when they heard what the shepherds said to them. Mary hid these things in her heart; she continued to think about them. Then the shepherds went back to their sheep, praising God and thanking him for everything that they had seen and heard. It was just as the angel had told them.

When the baby was eight days old, he was circumcised, and he was named Jesus. This name had been given by the angel before the baby began to grow inside Mary.

JESUS IS PRESENTED IN THE TEMPLE

The time came for Mary and Joseph to do what the law of Moses taught about being made pure. They took Jesus to Jerusalem to present him to the Lord. It is written in the law of the Lord: "Give every firstborn male to the Lord." Mary and Joseph also went to offer a sacrifice, as the law of the Lord says: "You must sacrifice two doves or two young pigeons."

SIMEON SEES JESUS

A man named Simeon lived in Jerusalem. He was a good man and very religious. He was waiting for the time when God would help Israel. The Holy Spirit was in him. The Holy Spirit told Simeon that he would not die before he saw the Christ promised by the Lord. The Spirit led Simeon to the Temple. Mary and Joseph brought the baby Jesus to the Temple to do what the law said they must do. Then Simeon took the baby in his arms and thanked God:

"Now, Lord, you can let me, your servant,
die in peace as you said.
I have seen your Salvation with my own eyes.
You prepared him before all people.
He is a light for the non-Jewish people to see.
He will bring honor to your people, the Israelites."

Jesus' father and mother were amazed at what Simeon had said about him. Then Simeon blessed them and said to Mary, "Many in Israel will fall and many will rise because of this child. He will be a sign from God that many people will not accept. The things they think in secret will be made known. And the things that will happen will make your heart sad, too."

ANNA SEES JESUS

Anna, a prophetess, was there at the Temple. She was from the family of Phanuel in the tribe of Asher. Anna was very old. She had once been married for seven years. Then her husband died and she lived alone. She was now 84 years old. Anna never left the Temple. She worshiped God by going without food and praying day and night. She was standing there at that time, thanking God. She talked about Jesus to all who were waiting for God to free Jerusalem.

JOSEPH AND MARY RETURN HOME

Joseph and Mary finished doing everything that the law of the Lord commanded. Then they went home to Nazareth, their own town in Galilee. The little child began to grow up. He became stronger and wiser, and God's blessings were with him.

Our Family Traditions

What traditions does your family have during the Advent season? Do you set up a nativity scene, deliver cookies to neighbors, or hang a wreath on your door? Make a list and discuss how each tradition reflects Jesus' character or celebrates His coming.

TRADITION

_____

_____

_____

_____

_____

_____

_____

_____

_____

MEANING

_____

_____

_____

_____

_____

_____

_____

_____

_____

_____

_____

_____

Advent Activities for the Whole Family

There are so many ways to think about Jesus and show His love to others during the Advent season. Choose one or more of these ideas to do as a family.

1. Create a nativity scene out of LEGO or Play-Doh. Then use your scene to act out the story of Jesus' birth.
2. Choose a gift for a family in need from the holiday catalogs of a charity, such as Samaritan's Purse or Compassion International.
3. Sort through your toys and clothing, and donate items in good condition that you're done with.
4. Go caroling at a retirement home.

5. Make a red, green, and white paper chain, and write the names of Jesus from the Bible on it. Hang the chain on your wall, use it to decorate a mantel or shelf, or wrap it around the Christmas tree.

6. Volunteer to help decorate for the holidays at a retirement home, women's shelter, or other community organization.

7. As a family, practice and sing a Christmas song at a holiday celebration or church service.

8. Memorize a scripture from the Advent Bible reading plan on pages 56–57.

9. Purchase baby clothes and supplies, and donate them to a pregnancy care center.

ABOUT THE AUTHOR AND ILLUSTRATOR

Sarah Young, author of the bestselling 365-day devotionals *Jesus Calling*® and *Jesus Listens*®, was committed to helping people connect with Jesus and the Bible. Her books have sold more than 46 million copies worldwide. *Jesus Calling*® has appeared on all major bestseller lists. Sarah's writings include *Jesus Calling*®, *Jesus Listens*®, *Jesus Always*, *Jesus Today*®, *Jesus Lives*™, *Dear Jesus*, *Jesus Calling*® *for Little Ones*, *Jesus Calling*® *Bible Storybook*, *Jesus Calling*®: *365 Devotions for Kids*, and more, each encouraging readers in their journeys toward intimacy with Christ. Sarah believed praying for her readers was a privilege and God-given responsibility and did so daily even amidst her own health challenges.

Connect with Jesus Calling at:
Facebook.com/JesusCalling
Instagram.com/JesusCalling
Youtube.com/JesusCallingBook
Pinterest.com/Jesus_Calling

Sally Wilson is a freelance designer and illustrator living in Northamptonshire, England. After graduating from Manchester Metropolitan University with a degree in textiles, Sally was an in-house designer for a major greeting card company before branching out into the wonderful world of freelance. Sally's work has appeared in books and on cards, gift wrap, and textiles.

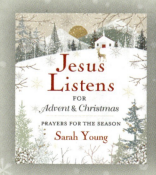

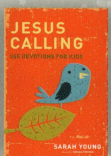
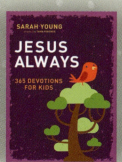